Ready, Set, Succeed!

This book is dedicated to Rick, for always believing...

Ready, Set, Succeed!

A guidebook for the successful job hunter

By Donna L. Wylie

Wylie Media, Colorado;

Sales@WylieMedia.com

INTRODUCTION

This book isn't meant to be used as a guide on how to choose a career. There are many excellent books on that topic alone. Rather, this book is meant as a practical method for getting the job you want.

I will also include some examples of my own experiences. They are offered simply for you to use, learn from, and perhaps smile at.

On to the hunt!!

"WHERE DO YOU GET OFF TELLING ME WHAT TO DO?"
(About the Author)

Why should you listen to ME? What do I know? For one thing-I've been there! I have worked for over three decades, on one side of the desk or the other. Most of that time was spent in a variety of retail management jobs, but I also have plenty of experience as a "worker bee." I've seen it all—the good, the bad, and the ugly! I know what employers are looking for, and what potential employees do to win the race. I've been a participant, on both sides of the table, in more interviews than I care to remember. As a manager, I interviewed hundreds of people over the years, for positions that ranged from part-time to management. In every case, while I knew basically what I wanted and needed, in the end it was personality not talent that won me over. The same was true of cases where I was the one being interviewed. When talents were similar, what won out was the personality type that fits best with that particular employer and job.

I also worked (one of my many hats) as an employment counselor, where I learned valuable "tricks of the trade." Employment counselors garner outrageous sums for doing what ANYone (with a little information) can do on their own! I didn't last long in that job because I felt like I was robbing people!

I have always wanted to do something for all the people who need good employment, but can't afford to pay a professional to help them obtain it. So here, in one neat little reference package, are all the "tricks" You will ever need to know to be your own employment counselor.

Everything you need to win is already inside of you, just waiting to be released. Ready—Set—Succeed!!

"Ready…"

GETTING THE INTERVIEW

Before you start out on a trip, you usually do some planning. Where to go, what to see, where to stay. It is just as important to plan for your career-hunting trip! So, to avoid "road closures", potholes and detours, take the time to fully prepare for this journey.

Deciding your future can be overwhelming and intimidating to the point of paralysis. Like any other major task, it is more manageable if you break it into smaller pieces. I know people have been asking you "what do you want to be when you grow up?" since age five, but forget all that for now. First let's just concentrate on what you like to do. That's easy enough, isn't it? Go to any high-priced employment agency and that's what they'll do—find out your likes and dislikes and try to fit you into a career "slot." But you certainly don't need someone else to tell you all that. In fact, any time you involve another person there is a natural tendency to try to impress them. So all you really need is a pen, paper, and some common sense and honesty.

Divide your paper in half. Label one column "like" and the other "dislike" (or, I use a smile face and a frown face, just for fun). Now start making your list. If you have had a few jobs, critique each one. If you have never worked, then list what you liked and disliked about school, hobbies, clubs etc. In fact, even if you've held a ton of jobs, it would be wise to also list hobbies and volunteer work. After all, what we do in our leisure time is generally a more accurate barometer of our likes and dislikes than our choice of employment. For example, we may work as a computer technician, but spend our free time teaching adults to surf the internet. Or we may take a management job for the pay, but volunteer at an animal shelter on our days off.

Sometimes what we want to do means we have to make some monetary concessions. I work in customer service now, rather than management, because it brings me closer to what I truly enjoy—helping people. In my free time, I do other things I enjoy—write and work on developing classes for my company and a local college.

So don't discount the value of "fun" activities in helping you choose a career path.

When you are writing your list, remember—grammar, spelling, and neatness don't count! But honesty is a must. Forget the politeness rule in this case and be brutally honest. No one will see this so don't worry about hurting feelings or impressing anyone.

Here's an example. Let's use a character we'll call "Susan". She's a collection of numerous people I have met and counseled over the years. Here is what her chart might look like:

Job	Liked	Disliked
Waitress	Talking to people	On my feet, Heavy trays, Low pay
Gas Station Attendant	The people, easy work, learned about cars	Winter outdoors! Always smelled like gas
Retail Manager	Being in charge, the fast pace, independent work, sense of accomplishment	Upper mgmt Never satisfied & never gave praise, working nights
Customer Service Rep	Helping people, solving problems	Office politics!

So what does this chart tell us? Take a good look and see if you sense a pattern. Obviously, this person likes working with the public. It's a short list, so you can't tell much more. That's why your list should be as extensive and detailed as possible. If I had listed more examples from Susan's experience, you would have seen more patterns. **Patterns are what we are looking for**. Things like: Do you like working with people, or alone? Do you feel more comfortable giving orders, or taking them? Do you like a fast pace? Does pressure to perform bring out the best in you? Do you prefer a certain age group?

The more questions you can ask—and answer—the clearer your picture will be. You know—the picture of what you want to be "when you grow up." Once you have some idea of that, you can look for jobs in that field. For example, someone who is outgoing and enjoys talking to people might be a good salesperson, host/hostess, human resources or public relations employee, etc.

If you need help matching your personality and qualities to a particular career field, there are numerous books you can consult. One that immediately comes to mind is the time-tested "What Color is Your Parachute", but there are many other excellent books to choose from.

It may take researching some jobs as well. For instance, Susan liked children and thought teaching would be a good career for her. However, through her classes and part-time jobs, she discovered that she found public education very restrictive. But she had years of satisfaction and fulfillment as a church school teacher where the rules were far more flexible (and you were allowed to pray when the kids got out of control!).

So spend some time researching the field you are interested in. If you are having trouble deciding, you may even want to visit a company or two and talk to the people who work the job(s) or field(s) you have selected. You can always say you are researching for school, if you feel you need a cover. The important thing is to get as many facts as you can.

Talk to employees, rather than managers, whenever you can. The management has to give you the "company line"—whether they know why you are there or not. The employees—the people in the trenches—will be more honest about how they feel about the company. Ask them how they like their jobs, the company, their boss. Take what they say with a grain or two of salt, however. The opinions will vary widely, colored by each individual's experience. Use what you hear to get an overall view of the company.

Don't forget the internet when researching companies. It's usually as easy as typing in www.thecompanyname.com. Gather some facts and figures for use when you interview, or in your phone conversations. Answer for yourself, the "why do you want to work here" question. Is it their company philosophy? Their longevity? The benefits? Come up with as many reasons as you can. Order them from most to least important (what You consider important) in case you can only mention one or two.

Once you have chosen your career field, it's time to move to the next step in your journey. Getting an interview!

"Set..."

Want Ads are probably the worst way to job hunt! As soon as the ad comes out, applicants start lining up. So while you may still wish to use want ads (cover all your bases!), there are better ways to get interviews, number one being:

THE PHONE CALL. Aka—"The Cold Call"

Why is this called the "cold call"? In the business world, a "cold call" is one where the party you are calling has never heard of you. They don't know you, they're busy, they have no time to waste on social niceties. You have to "warm them up"--Introduce yourself in such a way that they at least are willing to listen to your whole pitch (as long as it's brief and relevant!) Not an easy task in a 2-minute (if you're lucky!) phone call. And, as salesmen the world over know—there is a pretty high failure rate to cold calls. Think of the telemarketers you've hung up on before they got two sentences into their "have I got a deal for you" speech! I'm not telling you this to discourage you. Far from it! I am telling you this so that you don't give up after the first call. Or the first Ten calls. Hang tough, keep dialing, and don't forget the number one rule—Be Prepared!

It's vital that you take some time to pratice before making the call.

First - Write a list of your talents. Be brief and specific. DON'T be shy!! This is your "sales pitch", your way to convince a prospective employer to "buy."

DON'T SAY:
"I love people." (That phrase is so over-used, it makes employers cringe!)

"I'm a great Administrative Assistant." (That's an opinion)

"I'm a great employee." (Another opinion--How do they know you're great?)

DO SAY:
I have an excellent record of customer satisfaction!

"I type 80 words per minute." (Use facts and figures whenever possible)

"I'm always on time and my work history is excellent."

Second - Make a list of the companies you want to call. Use the phone book. The local Chamber of Commerce usually has a list of the top employers in town. Or write down names of companies you see as you travel around town. I used to use a 5x7 notebook, and write one company per page. That left room for notes. Be sure to write down the complete address, zip code included, for later reference (writing follow-up notes). You can use whatever works best and is portable.

Third - Prepare your script! Write down exactly what you will say, word for word. Actors have scripts. No one needs to know you are reading. Practice your lines before you call. A script will help you sound confident and believable. Remember, as mom always said, you only get one chance to make a good first impression!

(NOTE: See Appendix A for a good, all-purpose script outline that you can copy and use)

The best opening line I've found is "Good morning/afternoon (etc.). May I talk to the person who hires your _____(secretaries, administrative assistants, customer service representatives, brain surgeons etc.) ?"PAY ATTENTION to the answer! Write it down in that notebook. Be sure to get the receptionist's name also—they can be your best ally. Ask for spelling of names. You'll want to spell and/or pronounce them correctly. Remember—success is in the details.

Then say:
"Thank you, Ms. Jones (receptionist). Would Mr. Smith (person who does the hiring) have a moment to speak now, or would tomorrow morning be best?" (This is known as the "Yes-Yes approach"--more on that a little later.)
Always use surnames whenever you are given both a first and last name. It sounds more respectful. First names sound familiar. So the rule is, always use surnames Unless you only have a first name.

What if the person isn't available?

Say "When will Mr. Smith be available?" Leave your name and number if asked, but try to find out (Gently!) when the person will be in. If you are asked if you wish to leave a message on voice mail, by all means , say YES! When you get the voice mail, leave a brief "sales pitch" with three quick reasons to hire you. Something like:

"Mr. Smith, my name is Barb Green. I am an experienced Administrative Assistant. I type 80 words per minute, take dictation at 100 words per minute, and am adept at client relations. I would like to work for Zenon Corporation because you also have a proven record of success. I'm sorry we weren't able to talk today, but I will call you back the end of the week, or you may reach me at 555-5555. I look forward to hearing from you."

BOOM! In less than a minute, you just told Mr. Smith who you were, why he should be interested in you, why you are interested in His company, and set a follow-up date with a way to reach you. POWERFUL STUFF!!!

Had you been able to speak to Mr. Smith in person, you would have used a similar approach with **one major difference.** In sales, we call this the :

"Yes-Yes Approach"

You get through to Mr. Smith. Here's how the conversation goes:

You: Hello, Mr. Smith. My name is Barb Green. I am an outstanding Administrative Assistant, looking to have a career with an excellent corporation like Zenon. I type 80 words per minute, take dictation at 100 words per minute, and am experienced in client relations. I would like an opportunity to meet with you and discuss my qualifications. **Would Tuesday be best? Or is Thursday more convenient for you?"**

That last sentence is very important! It's what we call the "yes-yes approach." It gives the person a choice—between "yes" or…"YES!" You can't lose! If he says he doesn't have time this week, or he won't be available until next week, persist! Gently! Say "would next Thursday be acceptable? Or shall we make it the following week?" Always give two choices—Yes or Yes. He may say Thursday isn't good, but Friday is acceptable. Fine! It's alright to switch to a different day. The point is to get the interview!
Don't push Too hard. If he really doesn't have any openings, he'll tell you. Believe him BUT ask if you can send him a resume. Confirm the address and the spelling of his name. Thank him for his time and tell him you will be sending the resume out right away. Tell him you hope to be able to talk to him in the near future, and end the conversation. When you send the resume, be sure to mention the phone conversation in the cover letter, and thank him again for his time. (Another of mom's rules—politeness pays!)

Be sure to have your resume, and a sample cover letter, all prepared and ready to send. Wouldn't it knock their socks off to get your resume within 5 minutes of the time you hang up! If you become really adept, you can practically have it in their hands as you hang up!
If you have a computer, you can store the documents for fast and easy changes. You can also fax right from the computer. If you don't have a computer-borrow

one! You'll also want to have your resume saved on a CD or flash drive, to be sure you'll have it even if your computer crashes! You can never be too prepared.

What if you just can't talk to anyone?

You still want to thank the receptionist. Remember—the receptionist can be your best friend or your worst enemy. Start making friends right away. If you got a name of the person who hires, but you just can't get through, even to his voice mail, ask the receptionist if you can send a resume to Mr. Smith's attention. If she says they aren't hiring, say "I can certainly understand that. Zenon is one of the best companies in town. I would like to send a resume so maybe I can get in line for an opening." A little flattery is good!

You can also try calling back the next day and asking for Mr. Smith by name. When asked what this is in relation to, you can say you are "following up on a question regarding a job." That's true and it's often enough to gain you immediate, unquestioned access to Mr. Smith.

Record any/all information in your notebook/PDA/etc so you remember who you talked to, when and what the outcome was. The date is especially important. Then flag that page, so you'll remember to follow-up later. I use small post-it notes and jot a follow-up date on the part that sticks out of the notebook. You can also flag it electronically and maybe even set an alarm to prompt you when it's time to follow up!

Give Mr. Smith time to receive and read your resume. Not too long—you don't want him to forget. Try to get a resume in the mail to him the same day you called. If they will give you a fax number, even better! You can send your resume right away. In this case, be sure to use plain white paper. Those fancy papers and colors come across as "muddy" or worse when you fax them. I once had a client who had her resume printed on blue paper with soft pastel clouds. Lovely to look at but Horrible to fax! It came out on the other end looking like something had been spilled on it!

If you want to get an idea of how your resume will come across the fax line, make a photocopy and take a good hard look at the result. Is it crisp, clean, easy to read? If not, go back and reprint it on plain white paper. Here is where having your resume stored on a CD or flash drive is not only handy, but vital. This way, it can easily be reprinted and/or modified quickly.

I don't advise emailing your resume as an attachment unless you are computer savvy AND you know what word processing program the company uses. When you email something like a Word document, it must be in a format their computer can read or the result will be very Unimpressive gibberish!

Now call back. Ms Jones (the same receptionist) answers. The conversation goes something like this:

"Good morning, Ms. Jones! This is Barb Green. I'd like to speak with Mr. Smith. Is he in this morning, or would this afternoon be better?"

With any luck, your familiarity with everyone's name gains you access to Mr. Smith, no questions asked. If you aren't that lucky, still proceed confidently. Nothing sells better than confidence—belief in your "product." If you don't feel that way then—as they say—"fake it 'till you make it!"Pretend you are confident—eventually you will be!

If Ms. Jones asks what this is about (don't get mad—remember, that's her job. And she's good at it or she wouldn't have been hired), tell her this is in reference to a call you made last week. Again, this may be general enough to gain you access to Mr. Smith. Don't give more information than is necessary. Here is where the script is so important because it will help you keep to the point.

Once you get to Mr. Smith, you have two choices. If this is your first conversation, proceed as outlined above. If you had talked to Mr. Smith previously, then you want to follow up on the resume you sent him. Say:

"Good morning, Mr. Smith. This is Barb Green. I know you're busy, so I won't take more than a minute of your time. I was wondering if you had time to glance at my resume. You know, I'm highly interested in talking to you about a career with Zenon Corporation. I think my skills would benefit you. As I said, I'm an accomplished administrative assistant. If you don't have any current openings, perhaps we could discuss my qualifications for future openings. **Is This week good for you? Or would next week be better?" ("Yes-Yes")**

What if you don't get through to Mr. Smith?

That's alright--ask for his voice mail again. Leave a message with the same wording as above. End with how he can reach you--every way you can think of: phone, email, message machine, cell phone. This information should be on your resume also, so you don't have to depend on him to jot down the numbers. Tell him, "as I listed on my resume, there are a variety of ways you can reach me." Be sure to ask the "yes-yes" question--"I would like to set up a time to meet with you this (or next) week. Please let me know whether Tuesday or Thursday would be best for you."

(NOTE: As a general rule, Mondays and Fridays are not the best days for interviews. Mondays, people are usually busy getting into the work week. By Friday, they often have their attention more on finishing the week's work, and on the coming weekend, than on interviewing potential employees. Of course, if the employer chooses one of these days, say YES!)

ALWAYS put in the "yes-yes" phrase!

I can't stress the importance of the "yes-yes" approach enough. You MUST sell your "product." That product is YOU! Think of the sales approaches that worked with you, where You bought the product. What enticed you to buy? Wasn't it the belief the sales people had (or, made you think they had) in their product? Their air of confidence--that "of-course-you-want-this" attitude." Wow!" you think. "Is that actor convincing! I want that dog food and I don't even own a dog! "Now that's selling!

When selling yourself, you MUST project confidence—whether you feel it or not!! That's the hardest part. And that's why a script comes in handy. When you write your list of talents, be sure to get your family and friends to help. It's often easier for other people to sing your praises.

GO!

Okay, you have the interview. Here are a few pointers for the important day. Some of them may seem trivial or picky, but remember—attention to detail is what will make you stand out! I'll give you the list first, then go into the details.

- **Dress up.**
- **Don't over-do cologne.**
- **Arrive early.**
- **Be prepared-pens, copies of your resume, references and job history.**
- **Bring ID-driver's license and Social Security card.**
- **Give a firm handshake when meeting the interviewer(s).**
- **Don't sit down until asked to do so.**

Dress up! For men this means a suit and tie; for women a suit or dress (nothing too short, and no plunging necklines, of course). It doesn't matter if you are going for a job in a warehouse. ALWAYS dress up. It shows respect and class. If you are uncertain about how to dress, you may want to check the bookstore or library for books on this specific topic. If you can't afford to dress up, you may want to check an organization called "Dress for Success" (www.dressforsuccess.org). According to their web site: " Dress for Success is a not-for-profit organization that helps low income women make tailored transitions into the workforce. Each Dress for Success client receives one suit when she has a job interview and a second suit when she gets the job." Check the web site for details. Unfortunately, there is no similar program for men. However, you can sometimes find nearly new suits at thrift stores. Have them professionally cleaned and that used suit can look like new at a fraction of the cost.

Be sure any cologne is light and appealing — nothing heavy or musky. If in doubt—go without! A good deodorant and that nice "soap and water" scent is all you need. Better to be subtle than to risk a scent that reminds the interviewer of someone they hate! That also happens! I once had a teacher who couldn't stand the smell of lavender because it was his mother-in-law's favorite scent. Much as we would like to think we are above such crass judgments—we aren't! Because scent is subliminal, people may find themselves disliking someone without being able to understand why. So—play it safe and either go without or wear a "positive" scent. Vanilla is a good scent—it has that homey, baked - goods kind of memory. Soap and water and baby powder says "clean". Lemon is cheerful. Whatever you wear, Don't overdo! I have talked with people (men and women) whose cologne was so strong it made my eyes water! Naturally, I was in a hurry to conclude the interview—NOT the effect you want!

Arrive at least 10-15 minutes early. This shows eagerness and excitement about working for that company. Prospective employers like that. I never hired anyone who arrived late. My feeling was, if they were that uncaring Before they were hired, what would they be like once they got the job?

Forget the "too thin or too rich" philosophy—I think **you can never be too prepared**! Always be sure you have a pen and pencil with you. Take a copy of your resume, just in case the interviewer can't locate yours in the pile (it happens!). Also take any additional information such as lists of references or any licenses the job requires. You may want to place any additional paperwork in a folder (an inexpensive manila file folder will do, as long as it's clean). This gives the impression of organization. As I learned in college, packaging is everything! It often means the difference between an "A" and a "B". Or, in this case, the difference between getting hired or not getting hired.

Be sure you have your driver's license and social security card (or alternate forms of ID) with you. Just in case the employer wants to hire you immediately (that also happens!), you'll be all prepared with the necessary papers to complete the I-9 form. And it will impress and amaze your future boss.

When you meet the interviewer always shake his/her hand. Firmly—not a bone crusher, just a nice firm grip. This gives the impression of confidence (whether you Feel it or not!). If you are worried about the "sweaty palm syndrome", take a tiny container of baby powder with you and dust on just a dab before the meeting. Not only will your hand be drier—you'll also have that subliminal "clean-cut, sweet, innocent" (Positive) scent.

This is a very subtle move, but extremely important—Don't sit down until you are invited to do so. This may sound silly, but it isn't! Rather, it sends an important unspoken message to the interviewer. It says "you're the boss, I'm here to do what you want." Employers like that. It gives the impression of respectfulness and courtesy. Again, the effect is subliminal—the interviewer will like you without exactly knowing why. The reason this is so important is because most interviewers form a judgment within those first brief moments. Much of their opinion is based on nonverbal clues like your appearance, handshake, scent, and body language.

When talking with the interviewer, always listen attentively. Lean forward slightly in your chair. This gives the attitude of interest. Never interrupt, but ignore it if they do-- it's one of the marks of status (bosses interrupt employees far more than the reverse). So by ignoring and allowing any interruptions on their part (but curtailing your own), you are again reinforcing the message that you know who is in charge. Bosses like that—a lot! It gives them the impression that you will be an employee who will do what they ask without arguing or disagreeing constantly.

In case you hadn't noticed, these tips are all designed to form a positive impression in the mind of the interviewer. Employers are looking for employees who will be dedicated, hard-working, and loyal (to name a few of the qualities bosses look for). Of course you ARE all these things, aren't you? So make sure the employer knows that! Show them what a hard worker you will be by working hard at impressing them.

Some Tough (but Standard) Interview Questions:

When people find out I've conducted a lot of interviews, invariably, the first question they ask is "WHY do All interviewers ask the same stupid questions? What are they looking for?"They look to me because I've been there. So I must know the reasons behind the questions, the "secret handshake", so to speak, of bosses' inner thoughts. After all, if you can understand, you can be better prepared. Standard questions, "proper" answers.

Would you be shocked to know that the "inside answer" to the "secret question" is a simple "I Don't Know!"? That's right—most employers really have no idea what the "right" answer is! They just know if they like your answer when they hear it! Often, they are asking the "standard" questions because they have never been taught how to interview. So they rely on form questions and their own "gut-level" response to the replies. So then, you might ask, what "good" are the questions? And how on earth can you provide the "right" answer if there ISN'T one?

There ARE some guidelines that influence even the most clueless boss, and that can assist even the most baffled applicant. Whether they are aware of it or not, most employers are looking for attributes that can't be put into words. So the answers to the questions aren't the main thing. What "sells" (or-doesn't!) are the non-verbals—attitude, demeanor, approach. In fact, what you don't say, or what is said "between the lines" is often the determining factor.

Intimidating isn't it? But let me remove some of the mystery. Here is what I was actually looking for, as a manager, when I followed the script of standard questions:

Attitude—Does the applicant take the questions seriously without asking "why"? That tells me they will probably also take orders and directions well. While I wasn't looking for a "yes-man" (er—make that "yes-PERSON"!), I also wanted to avoid the type of person who needs a Good reason before they will complete a task.
Don't get me wrong—I always had a good reason for any directions I gave. I just didn't always have a lot of time to explain the lightening-fast connections my mind went through when deciding on a course of action. When there is time, I explain. When there isn't, I need immediate acceptance!

Personality—Does the applicant's personality "fit"?
In other words, will I be able to get along with them? And—just as important, is this the type of person I want representing my company? Do they have a sense of humor? Compassion? Do they really appear to like people? (Everyone Says they do, but do they show that?)
Like attitude—even more so than attitude—this is a subjective judgment. Much as we, as employers, would like to think we are above such crass judgments, we are still human. As such, preconceived notions and prejudices sometimes influence us. It can often be so subtle that we aren't aware of it ourselves.

Honesty—Do I get the sense that this is an honest person?
Again, the clues are very subtle. Do they fidget when you ask them a question? Do they avoid eye contact? Do certain questions make them nervous? All employers want to hire an honest person. After all, statistics tell us that employees commit the majority of company theft. So relax, be yourself, and tell the truth.

Since you can't control how someone reacts to your personality, and since you don't want to have to play a part for the rest of your career—just be yourself. If the job isn't a good fit, it's best to find that out before you go to work at a place where you would be miserable.

So—having scared you let me now try to reassure and prepare you. Here are some classic examples of "standard" questions, and some "tricks" (yes, there are some!) on the best way to answer:

What are some of your weak points?

Ooh-ow!, you think. What are they asking that for? What a horrible question! And you're right. But there are some "good" answers. I would say "well, I'm a little over-ambitious when it comes to organizing things." The employer thinks that's a good thing. However, you'll have a tough time pulling that one off if you had to ask for a pen to fill out the application, or if you spent 10 minutes sorting through your briefcase to get a copy of your references. So it has to be something believable. I happen to really be obsessively organized.

Are you the opposite? Totally disorganized? Then say, "well I tend to just forget everything else when I'm helping a customer." Again, this will only work if you are applying for a job where the emphasis is on customer service. If the job is for a brain surgeon—well, you'd better be more organized!
If you are young and/or inexperienced, turn that into a positive "weak point." Say, "well I lack experience but that's why I'm looking forward to learning from the best." Flattery is always a good thing!

What are some of your strengths?

AW-Right!, you think. Finally! But be careful of this one. Keep your focus on the job you are trying to get and aim your answers in that direction. When I applied for a management job, I would say "I was always good at running the floor during the busy seasons." I might even add a personal note about how good it made me feel—NEVER say that you were good at something and then add a negative remark. For example, you WOULDN'T want to say "I was always good at running the store during the busiest seasons. Boy, was it a relief to see the slow times come!" Argh! You had it and you blew it!

 Speaking from experience, as one who tends to "babble" when I'm nervous, the Less said the better! It only seems like there is a 30-minute pause between your answer and the next question. Breathe-count to 10, smile and don't forget to lean forward slightly, as if in anticipation of the next "exciting" question.

Where Do You See Yourself in ___ Years?

This is my personal LEAST favorite question. No one has ever been able to tell me what answer they are looking for. All I hear is variations on the "I-don't-know-art-but-I-know-what-I-like" comment. Again, keep your focus on the job.

Are you applying for a position with a company that offers franchises? Then maybe you would want to reply, "I'd like to own my own store within 5 years." Are you applying for a position as a vet's assistant? Maybe you would say "I'd like to be a vet and I thought this job would help me gain valuable practical experience." Are you applying to McDonald's as a fry cook? Maybe you can respond, "I'd like to work my way up through the ranks until I can own my own restaurant."

Employers like to hear answers that say you will still be with their company, in an increasingly more responsible position. Just don't phrase it that exact way—tailor your answers and keep your eyes on the job you want to get.

The best answer I ever heard to this question (looking at it as a former manager) came from my husband. Ok, yes, I May be a little prejudiced. On the other hand—he got the job he was applying for. So I wasn't the only one he impressed.

The interviewer asked my husband the traditional "Where do you see yourself in 5 years" question. He told her he couldn't give her an answer until he got inside the company and started looking at all the possibilities! I loved that answer and so did she! Why? Because it implies he will be working for them soon (confidence) and that he is flexible enough to keep his options open.

What did you like most about your last job?

Don' t say, "going home"! Even if you hated your job, find something good to say about it. For example, I had a customer service job for two years where I absolutely hated the office politics. I must have liked something though, or I wouldn't have stayed there. So think-what attracted you to, or kept you at, your last job? For me, I really enjoyed the satisfaction of resolving tough customer issues--calming down angry people, helping frustrated ones, saving people who were really fed up with the company. That's a good thing to tell the interviewer. Remember to stick to the positive. DON'T say "the boss was a jerk, but I really loved helping customers"! Stick with the part about helping customers, and be ready to supply several examples if the interviewer asks.

What did you like least about your last job?

Careful! This isn't the water cooler, and the interviewer isn't asking because they haven't heard any really good gossip lately. Do not, repeat--do NOT air your grievances here! Ever! No Ifs, Ands or Buts! I don't care if you thought your last boss was the worst person in the world--do NOT badmouth either the company or the boss! It leaves the impression that you are a complainer. No company is perfect, the interviewer thinks. If he or she hires you, what tales will you be telling about this company 6 months down the road? So--once again, take a breath and keep it positive. You may want to say,

"I didn't feel there was enough opportunity for growth (or advancement)." Say you needed more challenge, better benefits, closer proximity to home.

Maybe you prefer to work in the city and your last job was located in a rural area. Or perhaps you want the perks that come from working for a bigger company--stock options, an on-site health club, etc. Be sure your answer fits the current employer. For example, if you say you need a job closer to home, and this company is a farther commute than the last one, that reason won't fly. So choose answers that make sense and fit the situation. This is why preparing ahead of time is so vital. You may not have the same response, even to the same questions, with another prospective employer.

Other "are they really trick questions" Questions:

Many employers want to "test your mettle" and will ask you "what if" questions. I was once applying for a position as a trainer. The interviewer asked what I would do if I had a class of new hires (it was a call center), and only an hour in which to get them ready to take calls. I thought a moment—Always take a moment to think (and breathe!) so it doesn't look as if you rehearsed your lines (this is supposed to be spontaneous, remember—your job is to be as prepared as possible without looking like you were!). Then I told the interviewer that I would teach the new hires customer service skills. And I told the why—I said "they can probably fumble their way through the computer systems, but without good customer service skills, the customers won't be patient and wait for them to fumble through." The interviewer actually said "good answer!"—Probably an interviewer faux pas. They aren't supposed to let you know if you got the question "right". Just a little game they play to maintain that control so important to bosses. So don't be concerned if you get no response to what you thought was a brilliant answer.

With that in mind, here are some examples of other "trick questions":

*What would you do in _____ situation? This is a tough one to prepare for. Keep in mind, the Interviewer often doesn't know what they are looking for! So just be as honest as possible. I usually give some general answer like "I would take a brief moment to assess the situation and then act in the best interest of the customers, company and employees." Some bosses are veteran interviewers and this type of generic response won't cut it. In that case, take another deep breath and try to come up with a more specific response. It's okay to ask for a more specific example—after all, all of your real-life experiences will be specific. One way to prepare for this question prior to the interview is to try and think of situations where you had a similar job, and jot down some examples of situations you handled. Here's another situation where honesty is the best policy if you get nervous and can't think. Feel free to say, "May I consult my notes? I took the liberty of writing down some examples of my past experiences." You may wish to just briefly mention that interviews make you nervous (no surprise there!) and you wanted to be sure you didn't forget an important point. As a manager, that kind of response would have scored big points with me. Why? Because it shows the person took time to prepare with some pertinent notes, and it shows they are honest.

*What would you do if you saw another employee stealing/cheating/etc? I always answer that I would speak to my direct supervisor. Companies want to know that you don't condone theft or cheating. NEVER imply that you would have to "know the circumstances"! Company policy (Everywhere!) is that dishonesty is not to be tolerated for any reason. No exceptions to this rule, if you want to get hired.

*Do you prefer working as a team or an individual?
How is the company structured? Pick the right response according to that.

*How would you handle an angry customer? This is a classic question in any business that has dealings with the public, so be prepared! The "correct" answer would be something like "I would listen courteously, remain calm, and keep my voice low and respectful. I would NEVER raise my voice or argue with the customer. I would show empathy and offer to repair the mistake in any way possible." Again, this is a time when you never say, "it depends on the situation"! That implies that you May want to disagree with customers—a definite no-no!

*Some questions they don't need to ask you (and what to do if they do):
Prospective employers shouldn't ask you things like:
Do you have a car? (unless the job requires that you do)
How will you get to work?
Are you planning on starting a family soon?
Will you be going back to school to finish your degree?
Do you have any illnesses?
Do you have any outside obligations that might interfere with your schedule?

What they are trying to find out is how available you are for extra hours, or how likely it is that things like Little League and dance class might interfere with your schedule. They shouldn't ask these things. It is your responsibility to adhere to your schedule— that is understood when you are hired. But no employer should be asking for "guarantees" before you are hired.

Be aware of the optional part on some applications that ask what your hobbies are, or what organizations you belong to—you don't need to answer. They aren't interested in you as a person—remember, they are looking at you as a potential employee. So I always put "safe" hobbies (if I fill that in at all)—things like needlepoint and reading. In other words, you probably won't want to list your devotion to coaching your child's baseball team. The employer may see that as a potential problem—after all, they think your focus should be on work. Unrealistic, perhaps, but a very real prejudice.

If I fill in the "organizations" part, I'd put down things like my membership in Honor Societies. Always look at your answers, as a prospective employer would view them.

IF THE EMPLOYER ASKS you a question that you wonder about—ask them! Say, "Can you tell me what the relevance is to the position I am applying for?" If they won't tell you, and the question makes you uncomfortable, maybe you'd be better off looking somewhere else anyway.

And—last but not least—The piece' de Resistance: "Why should I hire you?"

This is another one of those nebulous questions that leaves you gasping for air and fidgeting with your collar. And it's another one of those "I don't know art but I know what I like" kind of questions. In other words, as with most questions, the interviewer has no idea of the "right" answer--They just know if they like your answer or not.

 Whatever you do, don't answer this question by saying, "I don't know", or words to that effect. Here's a time when you want to take a deep breath (so you don't Actually gasp!), lean forward slightly, smile confidently and say with Utter conviction, "Because I believe I am the best person for the job! And I would like a chance to prove that to you."

You may want to add a few brief "reminders"—tell them again, what you already told them. "I have ___ years of experience as a _____, and just a sentence or two about your other qualifications. Close by adding "I will work hard to do the best job possible because I really want to work for this company!" Remember—flattery!

In other words, this is no time to be shy! Lay it on Thick! Because-think about it. Why should they hire you? They've been interviewing people all day—maybe for several days. At this point, you're one of a blur of names in a pile on their desk. Do you want the job? Then say so! Tell them, "because I want this job. And if you hire me, I'm going to do everything in my power to make you glad you did!"

WOW! That may make the interviewer do a double take--and that's exactly what you want! You want to stand out.

So if you're a shrinking violet, "aw shucks" kind of person, find a way to get past that. I can't stress enough, how important this is. Get someone to play-act with you, asking you potential interview questions. A strong finish can often put you ahead of the pack.

Of course, sometimes the employer means this question literally. What they are thinking, but not saying, is "why on earth are you applying for this job?"

Let me give you an example of what I mean. Richard was a soft-spoken, gray-haired man in his 60's. Trained as a minister, and now semi-retired from that profession, he showed up at the housewares store I managed, to apply for a job as a part-time cashier. You can bet I asked him the standard "why should I hire you?" question! What I wanted to know, but couldn't ask, was "why are you looking for work here?"

The implication is—you could do so much better, so why would you want this job? Employers are rightly concerned about this, because they all want to hire for the long term. Turnover costs money in time spent interviewing, and training. So good candidates may be discarded, if the employer thinks they wouldn't really like or want the job.

Fortunately for Richard (and, ultimately-for me), he understood what I was really saying was that he didn't fit my concept of the "cashier type". He gave me an explanation that made sense to me. And he did it all with deference and dignity. I liked that. He turned out to be a long-term, loyal and dependable cornerstone of our organization.

So I gained a valuable employee, and Richard won out over other applicants, all because he heard and responded to what I was really asking. Be sure to listen for the "message beneath the message" if you want to win the position.

The Grand Finale—"What Questions Do You Have For Me?"

Here's where it helps if you did you homework. You can now interject some facts about the company, along with a question. For example:
"Well, I know you have job sites in 3 cities. Will I be traveling to each site on a weekly basis?"
Notice the careful wording. First, I mention a fact about the company, to show the employer I want the job enough to research. With the second sentence, I let the employer know that I expect to travel for the job, and simply want to know the Schedule. It sounds better than saying "will I have to travel for this job?"That sounds reluctant.

 Other questions you might ask:

"I know that your business is building houses. What additional training would you suggest I look into, to be sure I am fully prepared for a career in this field?" This tells the employer that you are determined to enter this field, and want to be the best you can be!

"When may I follow up with you about your decision? Is the end of this week best? Or would the beginning of next week give you more time? Would you prefer that I follow up by phone, email, fax, or regular mail?"

This shows the employer you are interested and serious about wanting the job. It also includes the "yes-yes" phrase, so that you are sure of getting a positive response. And it shows confidence that of course they want you to follow up!

Now What?

PSHEW! The interview is over! BIG sigh of relief. You walk out the door, head home and figure you are done-right? WRONG! The fun, while not just beginning, is far from over.

The FIRST thing you want to do when you get home is send a follow-up letter. Ok—you can kick off your shoes, loosen your tie, change and get comfortable first while you think about what you want to say.

You can see some example letters in Appendix C, but here are some of the basics:

Thank the interviewer for meeting with you on _____ (date).
Tell them you are (VERY) interested in working for them, maybe throw in another fact or two about the company (For example: "I would like to work for_____, a solid, Fortune 500 company with a proven track record in the ____field".)
Give them a couple reasons why they should hire you (again). And close with how they can reach you, or a reminder of when you arranged to contact them.

Okay—you are almost done. Write the letter and mail it Right away. Be sure to keep a copy for yourself. Note the date (if any) of follow-up on your calendar.

A final note about organization, since it is SO important. You will want to develop some organized method of filing information and following up on interviews and letters. Get a file box, and a big wall calendar, some brightly colored pens, post-it notes, a spiral-bound notebook, index cards—whatever works for you. If you are not that organized—find a friend or relative who IS!!

Just like it was important to show up prepared for the interview, it is vital that you follow through. Use the calendar in Outlook, for example, or any calendar program that will send you "prompts"--reminders to follow up with a certain company on a certain day. This will only work, of course, if you check email daily.

Beware! A word of advice….Don't use your work email or calendar to send reminders to yourself about job hunting! No matter how careful you think you are, or how clever, there is always a chance that you will be discovered – and fired! You don't want to have to put that on your resume, do you?! And you don't want to have to be searching for a job while you're unemployed.

However you prepare, or organize, one thing is important—Do what you said you would! That means, if you told Mr. Smith you would follow up with him on Thursday—you'd better do it! This is the hard part. After all, it's been two whole days (or 3 or 4 or a week) since you last spoke to Mr. Smith. And, gee—if he really liked you, wouldn't he have called you? Don't bet on it! Mr. Smith is a busy executive. More importantly—He's already employed. So—who's got the bigger stake in follow-through?

Once again, you are going to prepare, even rehearse if necessary, before you make that follow-up call. Get your script, and your notes about what happened the first time you called. Nothing worse than calling the secretary by the wrong name or mentioning the wrong facts—"oops, that was Company B....."

(See Appendix A again, for a sample follow-up call script that you can copy for your own use.)

The Big Finish!

Here's the quiz, the final exam. You knew there would be one, right? Well, This quiz is hands-on! The grade is up to you. Will you make the grade and get a job? Or be left behind to repeat the course? It's all in your hands. Heady stuff, and a little scary, isn't it? But you can do it! Just follow the simple steps:

1) Ready—Prepare!
2) Set—make the call.
3) Go!—interview and follow up.

SUCCEED!!!—A Final Word (or two) of Advice

Remember—the biggest factor in your success will be organization! I just can't stress that enough. So here's where all that boy/girl scout training comes in handy!

Keep notes on everyone you contact (or don't contact). You may want to contact them later. Did they tell you they wouldn't be hiring for at least a month? Well-you know what to do! That's right—come home and put a big reminder on your calendar! You have no way of predicting today, what you may be doing in a month—or even 6 months—down the road. So always make a note to yourself. In this world of face-paced, use-'em-up-and-lay-'em off jobs, it pays to keep all your options open. One year, I got laid off from TWO jobs! I only had the second job for about 6 weeks. You can bet I was glad I had kept all my job leads!

You will also want to keep notes on every interview you go on. Come home and, while it's fresh in your mind, make notes on how you think the interview went, and maybe some notes on what you would do differently the next time you interview with anyone. Review these notes before your next appointment and see what applies in general. For example: "I think my jewelry was too flashy-the interviewer seemed distracted by all my bracelets." Simple enough to heed that hint and go without the bracelets the next time. Write down things that went well also. It's important that you find something positive, even if it's as simple as "I remembered not to sit down until I was invited to do so." Wow! That's great! Record that! It proves you were cool under pressure. It's also important to record what went well, so that you don't start thinking you are doing something wrong if you aren't getting hundreds of job offers. Remember—it's a big ocean and there are millions of other fish! And remember—sometimes there is seemingly no good reason why you don't get hired. The interview went well, you are highly qualified, but you don't get the job. Could be any number of reasons from the position is no longer available (company restructuring), to--they had someone else in mind all along (it happens!). So don't get discouraged. Remember that famous adage "if at first you don't succeed…."

So. That's it. The "magic" formula that employment agencies use. They combine marketing your talents with sheer numbers—get as many interviews as possible and someone is bound to hire you! It's a winning combination—if it weren't, there wouldn't be all those employment agencies, would there? But-before you spend money on the "experts", give it a try on your own. After all—as far as marketing, who knows your talents and abilities better than you? And the delivery and presentation of those talents just takes a little practice. For that, you have the scripts in the back of this book. Feel free to make as many copies as you need for your own use.

Take a deep breath, stand up straight, smile, and repeat after me: "I can do it!" Now get out there and **Succeed!**

Appendix A
The Phone Call Script

"The Call" Script

Good [Morning/Afternoon]_____(receptionist's name, if he or she gave it). May I speak to the person who hires your _____(job title)?

If you get through to the person who hires:

Write down their name!_____

Mr./Ms. _____, my name is _____. I am an outstanding _____.

I (3 talents!)_____,
_____,
and _____.

I would like to meet to discuss my qualifications with you. Would (Day) _____ be agreeable? Or would (Day)_____ be better?

 If they say they are busy this week:

Well, I can certainly understand that. _____ (company name) is an excellent company. Would next week be better for you? Perhaps _____(day) or _____(day)?

Don't push! If they are really busy, or not hiring, they will tell you. Then say:

I understand. A company such as _____ (mention something positive about the company-Facts and figures are BEST!), with _____ must already have a staff of excellent employees. I would certainly like to be considered; next time you have an opening. May I fax you my resume? Or would it be better to mail it to your attention?
Fax/Mail _____Attention:_____

Thank you so much for your time, Mr./Ms._____. I look forward to meeting you in the near future.

If you Don't get through to the person who hires, or the receptionist puts you off:

May I have that person's name so that I may send a resume to their attention?

If you get a name, WRITE IT DOWN !
_____Then, call back the next day and start with:

Hello, Ms./Mr._____ (receptionist's name). May I speak
to Mr./Ms. _____ (person who hires) ?

If asked what this is in relation to:

This is in relation to a job position.

STOP! Don't say anything else! Never give more details than you have to!

If the receptionist says the person isn't in, or isn't available:

Very well. I would like to be put into his/her voice mail please.

If the receptionist says they have no voice mail, or it's broken, and insists on a message:

I understand. However, it's important that I speak directly to Mr. /Ms.
_____. What would be the best way to accomplish that?

Make the receptionist your ally and follow her/his suggestions! If you really can't get around her questions, or s/he won't give you any information, ask her/his help:

 I'm an excellent _____, and I really want a chance to talk to someone about getting a job with your company. What would be the best way to accomplish that?

NOTE: I Wouldn't use this approach if the job you are applying for is receptionist! Always take any advice with enthusiasm and gratitude, whether you think it was helpful or not! Remember--the receptionist can be your greatest help, or your biggest enemy.

The "Follow-Up Call" Script

Good [Morning/Afternoon]_____(receptionist 's name). May I
speak to Mr./Ms. _____ ?

If the receptionist asks why or what this is in relation to:

This is in relation to a conversation Mr./Ms._____and I had last
week. STOP! Be polite, but don't give more details than you have to!

When you get the person on the phone:

Mr./Ms. _____, my name is _____. We spoke last week,
regarding a potential job with you as a _____.
I told you I would send you my resume and follow up with you today.

My resume details my abilities.
As you can see, I (3talents!)_____,
_____,
and _____.

I am still very interested in pursuing a career with _____
(Company name), and was hoping we could meet to discuss this. Would
_____(day) be agreeable? Or would _____ (day) be better
for you? If this works, great! Make the appointment and thank them for their time!

If the person still says "no openings":
Well, thank you for taking the time to speak with me. I would like to check back with
you in the future. Would you suggest that I call in a month? Or would it be better to call
in _____ (name a month 2-3 months down the road)?

If you get a date (even 2-3 months down the road) when you may call back, say:
Thank you so much for your time, Mr./Ms._____. I look forward to
speaking you in the near future.
If the person insists there are no openings and won't give a date, ask:

May I ask how long you keep resumes on file?
(NOTE THE LENGTH OF TIME!_____)

Thank you so much for your time, Mr./Ms. _____. I look forward to
perhaps meeting with you in the future.

If this was a company you REALLY want to work for, be sure to make a note on your calendar, to call them back just a month before they will be throwing away your resume. THAT follow up call will be similar to the above script, with the exception that you will say:

Mr./Ms. _____, my name is _____. We spoke in _____ (month), _____ (year), regarding a potential job with you as a _____.

You have my resume on file, but I would like to bring you an updated one. I am still very interested in pursuing a career with _____ (Company name), and was hoping we could meet to discuss this. Would _____(day) be agreeable? Or would _____ (day) be better for you?

Proceed as above, depending on the answer you get. Be sure to keep careful record of any dates or times you discuss, and if you say you will follow up, DO IT! This shows you are dependable, persistent, and conscientious. What boss wouldn't like that?

Remember—You CAN do it!!

Appendix B
Sample Cover Letters

Date
Name of Individual
Title
Name of Company
Street Address
City, State, Zip

Dear_____:

I am interested in applying for a position as a _____.
I have excellent skills as a _____ and have enclosed my resume for your
consideration.
If [Name of Company] would like to utilize my skills and experience, please contact me
at your earliest convenience for more information and/or an interview.

Thank you, in advance, for your consideration.

Very truly yours,

Your Full Name
Your Street Address
City, State   ZIP code
Your Phone Number
Your Email Address

YFN
Enc.

Date
Name of Individual
Title
Name of Company
Street Address
City, State, Zip

Dear Sir or Madam:

After seeing your store location being built in CITY, I was excited by the prospect of working for such a prestigious company as COMPANY NAME. I am currently managing the _____ store in CITY and would welcome such an opportunity to further my career in the computer field.

I have a strong retail background with both large and small stores. My experience includes purchasing, upgrades and repairs of all types of PCs. I am also well-versed in the traditional retail roles of hiring, training, store ordering and merchandising, and direct P&L responsibilities. During the month of July, my store was the only corporate location to show an increase over the previous year's sales. I myself was among the top earners as a commissioned salesperson.

I have a great interest in computers as a career. I have created a home network running Windows ____ and _____, in order to gain hands-on experience. I currently hold MCP certification in both _____ and _____. In addition, I am familiar with Windows _____ and most major software applications.

My retail management background, coupled with my experience in computers, would prove to be an excellent match with COMPANY NAME. My salary is negotiable. Past positions have been in the mid-to-upper ___'s.

I look forward to speaking with you soon.

Sincerely,

Your Full Name
Your Street Address
City, State   ZIP code
Your Phone Number
Your Email Address

Date
Name of Individual
Title
Name of Company
Street Address
City, State, Zip

Dear NAME,

I would like an opportunity to discuss the College Admissions Representative position you have available. I have an extensive background in sales and management, and enjoy dealing with the public. My strongest sales assets have always been my sincerity and honesty, coupled with my organizational skills.

I am currently working as a Quality Assurance Trainer in a call center, but it is not a career position and I find I miss the contact with the public that I was used to in my retail experience. I would welcome the opportunity to meet with you and discuss both the position, and my qualifications. Hopefully, we'll have a match and neither of us will need to look any further.

Please call me at your earliest convenience. You may leave a message if I am not in, and I will return your call as soon as possible. I look forward to meeting you.

Sincerely,

Your Full Name

Your Street Address
City, State   ZIP code
Your Phone Number
Your Email Address

Date
Name of Individual
Title
Name of Company
Street Address
City, State, Zip

Dear Sir or Madam;

 I am passionately interested in acquiring a career position in the networking field. What I may lack in desired length of experience, I more than make up for in creativity, intelligence, flexibility, and a drive to learn. I have recently acquired my MCP in both Windows NT Workstation 4.0, and NT Server 4.0, and I continue to study and work toward my MCSE. I am willing to start in an entry level/temporary position; because I am confident I can soon prove my worth.

My resume is attached for your consideration. Please call if you have any further questions, and to set up a time when we may talk.

I look forward to hearing from you soon.

Sincerely,

Your Full Name
Your Street Address
City, State   ZIP code
Your Phone Number
Your Email Address

YFN
Enc.

Date
Name of Individual
Title
Name of Company
Street Address
City, State, Zip

To Whom It May Concern:

Just when I had about given up hope of ever matching my sales ability with product integrity, your ad appears. I believe we have a team!

I am a highly organized, creative, customer-oriented salesperson with extensive sales and management experience, as well as phone experience. I sell best, those things in which I believe. I sell even better when the product I believe in is beneficial to the customer.

 I have long looked for a Career—not just someplace to take up space and collect a paycheck. I want to make a difference, make the world a better place, and – if I can get paid while doing so, well, that would be my idea of a dream come true! I would welcome the opportunity to meet with you and discuss both the position, and my qualifications. Hopefully, we'll have a match and neither of us will need to look further.

My resume is attached for your consideration. Please call me at your earliest convenience so that we may schedule a time to meet. Leave a message and I will return your call as soon as possible. I look forward to talking with you.

Sincerely,

Your Full Name
Your Street Address
City, State   ZIP code
Your Phone Number
Your Email Address

YFN
Enc.
Date

Name of Individual
Title
Name of Company
Street Address
City, State, Zip

Dear Sirs;

I am the trainer you are looking for! This job sounds tailor-made for me. I am an extremely organized individual, with a well-rounded background. I have worked in sales for many years. In addition, I have done public speaking in a variety of settings, and am comfortable in either large or small groups. I also have experience in training.

I am flexible and creative, able to adapt quickly to any situation. I originally trained to be a teacher, but left that field when I realized I enjoyed working with adults instead of children. In a previous position, I created an operations manual that was used in three local stores.

My resume is enclosed for your perusal. Of course, since resumes don't tell the whole story, I look forward to meeting with you in the near future. Thank you for your attention to this matter.

Sincerely,

Your Full Name
Your Street Address
City, State   ZIP code
Your Phone Number
Your Email Address

YFN
Enc.

Appendix C
Sample Follow - Up Letters

*NOTE: The follow up letter should be sent immediately after your interview!

Date

Name of Individual
Title
Name of Company
Street Address
City, State, Zip

Dear _____;

I wanted to take a moment and follow up on our interview of [date]. I thoroughly enjoyed our meeting and feel [Company Name] is an excellent organization.

I am looking forward to hearing from you soon to set up a second interview.

I am sure that my proven background in [experience example], coupled with my successful [experience example], combined with my [talent or experience example], would prove to be a good match with your company. Thank you in advance for your time and attention to this matter. Once again, the only question I have is "when can I start?!"

Sincerely,

Your name
Address
City, State, Zip
Phone number

Date

Name of Individual
Title
Name of Company
Street Address
City, State, Zip

Dear _____;

I would like to take a moment of your time, to follow up on our interview last week. I was curious as to whether you had made your hiring decision yet. I am still very interested in the position and believe we would work well together.

Once again, let me reassure you that I am confident I could learn any software you are running. I look forward to hearing from you soon!

Sincerely,

Your name
Address
City, State, Zip
Phone number
Email

Appendix D
Internet Resources

Career Counseling:

http://yellowpages.msn.com/BasicSearch.aspx   Type in "career counseling", and enter the City and State where you want to locate them.

Choosing your career:

http://www.careersonline.com.au/disc/   This takes you through a step by step process of selecting the career that's best for you.

Post a resume/search for jobs:

http://www.monster.com/; Probably one of the best-known job hunting sites, I actually have gotten hired from a lead off this site. It takes some time to post your resume, but is well worth the effort. This site has a counter, where you can see how often potential employers have viewed your resume. You can also have search results emailed directly to you.

http://flipdog.com; Like Monster, Flip Dog allows you to post an online resume, do job searches , and have the results directly emailed to you. I got more results from this site, but not as many actual leads as Monster. However, your results will depend largely on what jobs you are searching.

http://www.dice.com/;   This is an excellent resource for technical jobs. Like the others, you can post a resume online and have jobs emailed to you. If you are looking for technical jobs, I would recommend also posting your resume on the other sites I've listed, to increase your chances of finding a job.

http://www.msn.com/; has a general category "careers", where you can research various aspects of finding a job, including fling an online resume for employers to review. MSN also offers a free, online, email address via hotmail.com.

http://www.jobbankusa.htm; Since 1995, JobBank USA has provided a wealth of resources to job hunters and employers.

http://yahoo.com/; is another one that offers both information on careers, and a free online email address. Yahoo is my personal favorite, and one I have used in the past. I was able to file my resume online. A free home page allowed me to see how often it had been viewed by potential employers, on a daily basis.

There are other free email services out there, such as http://excite.com. I would recommend using as many different ones as you can find. The more places you post your resume, the better a chance you have at getting results.

AOL's home page (http://www.aol.com) has a "jobs" link where you can search by city and state. They also have a link to help you find your perfect job.

I generally use an alternate email address, rather than my personal one, on my resume. Sometimes, an online resume will generate a lot of response from employment agencies, or companies wanting to offer you services such as a resume review. If you want to take advantage, all well and good. But if you'd rather not…. then an alternate email address is like having a phone number just for the telemarketers. Keeps things on your private email address—well-private!

Remember, posting your resume online should just be one of the methods you use to job hunt. It isn't the only way, or even necessarily the best way (depending on what job you are looking for). So don't limit yourself.

General Search Engine:

http://www.google.com/; Hands down, the easiest search engine I have found. You can type in a phrase, like "how to choose a career", and Google will find you plenty of results! Most other search engines work best using just one or two key words.

Wylie Media, Colorado;
Sales@WylieMedia.com

www.ingramcontent.com/pod-product-compliance
Lightning Source LLC
Chambersburg PA
CBHW052012280526
45793CB00005B/954